CONTENTS

PREFATORY NOTE
OR
Advertisement concerning
THE AUTHORESS

'The Secret has spread so far as to be scarcely the Shadow of a secret now', Jane Austen wrote ruefully in 1813. Until then, she had endeavoured to keep her identity strictly concealed from the public.

Unlike many of her female literary contemporaries, from Fanny Burney to Madame de Staël, she shunned any form of fame or publicity – fearing, as she put it, to be made 'a wild Beast', to be stared at, and speculated about, like one of the zoo animals at the Exeter Exchange. Even after her 'Secret' had begun to leak out, following the modest success of *Pride and Prejudice*, she published her novels anonymously; and the prefatory note to the last, *Northanger Abbey*, was signed merely by 'The Authoress'.

In that note, or 'Advertisement', she apologised to her readers for the fact that changes in 'places, manners, books and opinions' had taken place since the work's inception. Even she, with her wit, observation, perception and imagination, could not have conceived of the changes which would take place over the next two hundred years – above all in the realm of manners. Prominent among these would be the extraordinary changes in the use of names. The woman whose most 'elegant' heroine, Miss Woodhouse in *Emma*, would disdain Mrs Elton's use of a gentleman's surname alone – 'Knightley', indeed! – would surely have been insulted to find herself, in the twenty-first century, commonly referred to as 'Austen'. Almost as bad, though certainly preferable, is plain 'Jane Austen': 'Let me not suppose that she dares go about "Emma Woodhouse-ing" me' the heroine of *Emma* reflects acerbically.

The solution adopted for the purposes of this little book is to follow her own lead, and refer to her, simply, as 'the Authoress'. We can only hope that 'England's Jane', as another great writer in the English language called her, with a love and respect beyond barriers, would understand, and forgive – and perhaps even laugh.

Chapter The First

MANNERS MAKYTH MAN —
AND WOMAN

If I could persuade myself that my manners
were perfectly easy and graceful, I should not
be shy.

Sense and Sensibility, Chapter 17

She had the comfort of appearing very polite,
while feeling very cross.

Emma, Chapter 14

This little guide is the outcome, ultimately,
of a correspondence between the Authoress
of several novels, including *Pride and
Prejudice, Sense and Sensibility* and *Mansfield
Park*, and her eldest niece – Anna Austen, of
Steventon Rectory, in Hampshire.

In the summer of 1814 Anna Austen (then aged twenty-one) approached her literary Aunt with a request for help with a novel set in contemporary Regency Society which she herself was attempting  to write. Over the next few months, as successive instalments were sent, edited, discussed and returned, the exchange of letters between Aunt and Niece was illuminating. While finding much to praise, in terms of character, dialogue and style, 'Aunt Jane' was constantly struck by one major deficiency: her young niece's apparent unawareness of the 'Manners', etiquette and social behaviour of the day.

> As Lady H. is Cecilia's superior, it would not be correct to talk of *her* being introduced; Cecilia must be the person introduced.

was one immediate response, followed soon after by

When Mr Portman is first brought in, he would not be introduced as 'The Honourable': *that* distinction is never mentioned at such times.

Other comments concerned language ('Bless my Heart!' for example, was 'too familiar and inelegant' a usage for a Baronet such as 'Sir T. H.') and the strict code of paying, and returning, morning 'Calls' ('Mrs F.', Anna was instructed, 'ought to have called at the Parsonage before Sunday'). Much of Aunt Jane's social guidance could be summed up in one telling directive:

Let the Portmans go to Ireland, but as you know nothing of the Manners there, you had better not go with them. You will be in danger of giving false representations.

By 'Manners', Anna's Aunt here denotes far more than the mere niceties of 'Please', 'Thank You', and 'Your Servant, Ma'am'. The word was applicable to every aspect of daily life – from dress and domestic arrangements, to the treatment of servants, and the proper way to encourage or deter an admirer. 'Manners Makyth Man' is, of course, the famous motto of Winchester College, where the Authoress's much-loved nephews were pupils; and it is no coincidence that, in a combined family joke and compliment, she gave the name of Winchester's revered headmaster, Dr Goddard, to the fictional proprietress of the modest little ladies' school in her novel of 1816, *Emma*. Manners are, indeed, the foundation of a civilised society; it is with good reason that members of the '*ton*' – those persons of rank and fortune who set the tone – are referred to as belonging to 'Polite Society'.

The codes of behaviour which govern daily life should not be confused with mere formalities. They are based on solid principles of courtesy, propriety and, most of all, regard for the feelings of others. When the heroine's young sister, in *Mansfield Park*, finds herself about to experience life in a great country mansion for the first time, she is daunted by visions of 'silver forks, napkins and finger glasses', but her fears are shown to be groundless: what she encounters at Mansfield is a household of 'cheerful orderliness', where 'everybody's feelings were consulted'. Too much polish, in either appearance or manners, is in fact the sign of a flawed character, throughout the Authoress's works; and more than one of her heroines is temporarily taken in by a man whose good looks and gallant 'address' are not supported by any inner qualities of principle, morality, or selflessness. Of 'shy' Edward Ferrars, in *Sense and Sensibility*, she writes,

> He was not handsome, and his manners required intimacy to make them pleasing.

None the less, in contrast to the rake Willoughby, with all his charms of 'air', and 'open affectionate manners', Edward proves himself a true hero – not least, through his selfless observance of Society's 'Rule' that no gentleman should ever break off his engagement to a lady.

Mr Knightley's kindness to a woman of inferior rank in *Emma* causes the heroine of that novel to reflect gratefully, 'He is not a gallant man, but he is a very humane one.' By the end of the novel she has learned some important lessons in distinguishing gallantry from humanity. The forms of manners which should be scrupulously observed are, invariably, those which contribute to the comfort, or dignity, of others: and this Emma comes to understand – with Mr Knightley's cool, plain-speaking assistance. Though a man of wealth, authority and rank, he has no interest in society's trappings, preferring to walk rather than use his carriage (that symbol of social status so revered by pushy Mrs Elton) and happier in sturdy leather gaiters than the immaculate evening dress in which the sly, ambitious clergyman Mr Elton appears with such evident delight – 'spruce, black and smiling'. In trying to educate her protégée Harriet in what constitutes 'a gentleman', Emma has been wholly misguided: Mr Elton, with his aptitude for 'gallantry' and 'charades' – that popular parlour-game of trickery and rhyming word-play – and his lack of rational values, is in fact far less 'gentlemanlike' than the honest, un-assuming yeoman farmer Robert Martin, whom Emma has initially dismissed as 'coarse' and 'clownish'.

Of course, there are many instances in which a degree of artfulness and pretence may be necessary, for the sake of good manners.

Not a "gentlemanlike manner"

Marianne Dashwood's disdain for the accepted codes of conduct, in *Sense and Sensibility*, can amount at times to rudeness, and even cause hurt: 'Upon Elinor therefore', the Authoress notes, 'the whole task of telling lies when politeness required it always fell'. Anne Elliot, in *Persuasion*, may be dismayed by her family's ridiculous respect for rank and titles, but even she is concerned by her sister's disregard for the established 'Rules' of precedence when calling on other family members – believing 'such a style of intercourse highly imprudent', through giving 'continual subjects of offence' between the parties. Certain formalities are best observed – as the Authoress endeavoured to impress upon her headstrong niece, Anna.

Only by understanding Society's strict 'Rules' is anyone – man or woman – in a position to break them. 'I dearly love a laugh', declares Elizabeth Bennet (perhaps the Authoress's own best-loved heroine) in *Pride and Prejudice*; yet, she adds, more seriously, 'I hope I never ridicule what is wise or good'. She is in many ways an unconventional female, happy to splash through muddy fields and climb stiles, to arrive looking 'almost wild', with 'blowsy' hair, at a rich neighbour's grand house. Yet, while possessing an irreverent sense of humour and the 'lively, playful manners' which come to delight arrogant Mr Darcy, she combines her high-spirited intelligence and independent attitude with a profound respect for every worthwhile principle of morality, and correct behaviour. She is self-possessed and undaunted when faced with the grim grandeur of Lady Catherine de Bourgh's mansion, Rosings, because she is wholly familiar with the codes of behaviour required there. It might perhaps be mentioned here that the Authoress herself was able to visit His Royal Highness The Prince Regent's palace of Carlton House, in 1815, without too many doubts as to her ability to cope with the honour and acquit herself, without disgrace, as a 'gentlewoman'. 'I am a gentleman's daughter', Lizzy asserts proudly, when questioned – with some impudence – by Darcy's aunt as to her family connections and background. By obeying the code of 'Manners' expected of a gentleman, or gentlewoman, with all the grace of courtesy and good humour which this implies, no one need fear social embarrassment.

As the Authoress's novels have shown, wealth and rank are no guarantors of good breeding. Some of her own, her family's, and her readers', greatest 'laughs' have been at the expense of self-important titled people: and though no supporter of radicalism in any form, she has always been happy to demonstrate a disrespect for those who value themselves on their birth, rather than any more genuinely honourable, or admirable, characteristics. At a time when some of the nation's finest have given their lives in the service of others, it is not for a Lady Catherine de Bourgh, or Sir Walter Elliot, to claim any innate superiority over their fellow man. Rules of precedence must, for the good order of society, be strictly observed in public; but in private most will sympathise with the Authoress when, mentioning two family friends in a letter of 1813, she wrote lightly,

I do not care for Sir Brook's being a Baronet, I will put Mr Deedes first, because I like him a great deal the best.

Certain words, recurring throughout her novels, should indicate to Anna, and the

"So evidently written by a Gentlewoman"

Authoress's other readers, which social attitudes are – in her opinion – really to be valued. 'Gentlemanlike' is prominent among them. Elizabeth Bennet's rebuke, 'Had you behaved in a more gentlemanlike manner', when refusing Darcy's first proposal of marriage in *Pride and Prejudice*, carries more weight than almost any other 'put-down' could, and is perhaps more efficacious in causing him to re-evaluate his own attitudes and social mores. For a lady to be termed 'elegant' is one of the highest forms of praise – indicating, as it does, the most desirable combination of good looks, good manners, good breeding and a gentle observance of Society's 'Rules', without ostentation or 'show'. A word with more doubtful applications, in the context of manners, is 'Ease': while Elizabeth Bennet is delightful for her 'easy, playful' approach to life, affected, self-congratulatory Mrs Elton is censured for possessing 'too much ease', in her behaviour towards others.

The validity of the Authoress's advice to Anna about not attempting to write of Ireland, given the difference in manners in different countries, was well borne out by her amused comment after a ball in 1804, at which one gentleman – though attached to a party of minor aristocracy – had contravened all the rules of manners: as she wrote,

> [After] eyeing me for some time . . . at last, without any introduction, [he] asked me if I meant to dance again. I think he must be Irish, by his ease.

Whether or not she appreciated this 'easy' and unconventional example of ballroom 'Manners', she did not state.

Every society has its 'Rules' – and where these contribute to good order, and the well-being of all, it is (on balance) as well to abide by them. At all events, it is necessary to be thoroughly acquainted with them: in the world of which the Authoress writes, a thorough understanding of the proper codes of conduct is the only rational recipe for happiness, in life, as in literature. A kind reader of *Mansfield Park*, Mrs Pole, has said, in the Authoress's praise, 'There is a particular satisfaction in reading all Miss A—'s works: they are so evidently written by a Gentlewoman . . .' She added

Everything is natural & . . . told in a manner which clearly evinces the Writer to *belong* to the Society whose Manners she so ably delineates.

It is hoped that Anna Austen, both in her life and her literary endeavours, benefited from her Aunt's advice. For all readers of the Authoress's novels, from *Pride and Prejudice* to *Persuasion* and *Northanger Abbey*, along with her other works, perhaps the following Rules of social behaviour may provide some guidance as to how to behave in 'Polite Society', with a deepened awareness of all the pleasures and hazards which the heroine of *Emma* summed up as 'compliments, charades and horrible blunders'.

Chapter the Second

THE FORMS OF INTRODUCTION

His indifference to a confusion of rank
bordered too much on inelegance of mind.
Emma, Chapter 24

You are not going to introduce yourself to Mr
Darcy?
Pride and Prejudice, Chapter 18

When the foolish clergyman Mr Collins, in
Pride and Prejudice, declares his intention of
introducing himself, uninvited, to the most
distinguished guest in the room, haughty, patri-
cian Mr Darcy, Elizabeth Bennet is horrified.
Though no respecter of rank, or fortune, she
possesses true 'elegance' of mind and manners,

and recognises when society's codes should, or should not, be respected. In this instance, she is in no doubt. As she endeavours to explain to her clergyman cousin, in vain, 'It must belong to Mr Darcy, the superior in consequence, to begin the acquaintance'. The patronising reproof which she receives from misguided Mr Collins is outweighed only by the dandyish 'put-down' which he – without even realising it – receives in his turn from Mr Darcy.

The Authoress herself, like her heroine Elizabeth, acknowledged society's codes and rules of precedence – even while laughing at them on many occasions. However foolish the social framework which Lady Catherine de Bourgh would term 'the distinction of rank' may be, it exists in all societies, of all eras; and only through a proper acquaintance with its structure can the wise or witty of either sex safely defy it, to anything but their own embarrassment. For those wishing to enter, or understand, the Authoress's social world as depicted in her novels, certain guiding rules may be of assistance.

Rule 1. Do not be presumptuous in offering introductions

When, and how, one person should be introduced to another is at all times a matter of great delicacy. It is for the 'superior in consequence' to indicate whether he or she wishes to permit the introduction of an inferior; and a third party, entrusted with bringing together any two persons in this way, must do so with caution. If the words 'Will you introduce . . . ?' are not forthcoming from the person of higher rank, there can be no further attempt to effect an introduction.

This 'Rule' can have some striking consequences – as the Authoress's novels frequently demonstrate. When Lady Catherine de Bourgh, in high dudgeon, calls on the Bennets in *Pride and Prejudice* to dissuade Elizabeth from marrying her nephew Darcy, she does not ask Lizzy to introduce her mother, and sits for some time in the presence of an awed Mrs Bennet, who has therefore not been granted permission to converse with her Ladyship in her own house. This, of course, is not 'good manners'.

A not dissimilar situation – on a lesser social

level – arises when Emma Woodhouse, out walking with her protégée Harriet in *Emma*, meets with the girl's admirer, yeoman farmer Robert Martin: Emma pointedly does not invite Harriet to introduce her friend, but stands apart, unspeaking and aloof, while the others respectfully converse.

The proper procedure for an introduction is conducted with more grace by Mr Darcy, when, on meeting Elizabeth Bennet in the environs of Pemberley, he asks her with impeccable courtesy,

Will you allow me, or do I ask too much, to introduce my sister to your acquaintance during your stay at Lambton?

Presumptuous as ever, Mrs Elton in *Emma* demonstrates her lack of 'good manners' by declaring when told of elegant, future landowner, young Frank Churchill's imminent arrival, 'I shall be very happy in his acquaintance', as though she, rather than he, would be bestowing the favour of her patronage.

"It is always the lady's right to decide
on the degree of acquaintance"

Rule 2. Respect a lady's reputation

Safeguarding the reputation of a lady is at all times a matter of the highest importance.

'It is always the lady's right to decide on the degree of acquaintance', declares Frank Churchill; and though he speaks as one who is involved in an elaborate social 'charade', concealing a secret engagement with Jane Fairfax, he is, on this point, correct. For fear of calling the good character of any female into question, it is proper for a gentleman, in public, to wait until he is greeted by the lady before acknowledging their connection, enquiring after mutual friends &c.

Rule 3. Do not attempt to bring friends of different ranks together

Many people in modern society may have acquaintances drawn from differing walks of life. This is entirely reasonable; but care must be taken in bringing them together. One of Emma Woodhouse's principal objections to visiting the humble Bateses is that to do so may involve her with 'the second rate and third rate', who are among their other callers.

Rule 4. Recognise the 'distinction of rank'

It is important to acknowledge that vast differences exist, even within 'Polite Society'. Different professions, for example, are regarded with different degrees of respect. While it is wholly acceptable for a gentleman to become a clergyman, a lawyer (like Emma Woodhouse's brother-in-law, John Knightley), a soldier, or, best of all in the Authoress's eyes, a sailor in Nelson's Royal Navy, other occupations are not deemed so suitable.

To live by trade, 'within sight of his own warehouses', as does the Bennet sisters' uncle, Mr Gardiner, is generally regarded as socially inferior; and doctors are in a particularly invidious position. The news that the well-liked doctor in *Emma*, Mr Perry, is setting up his carriage – the mark of a gentleman with an income of £500 or more per annum – is talked of with wonder in the novel; and in the Authoress's own life, the presence of a charming young physician, Mr Haden, as a regular guest at her brother Henry's parties in London needed some explanation. 'He is no Apothecary', she assured her sister, as a matter of some importance.

Advising her niece Anna on her novel, she had to make the social position of doctors clear, explaining,

> I have scratched out the introduction between Lord P and his brother & Mr Griffin. A Country Surgeon ... would not be introduced to men of their rank.

Rule 5. Become familiar with styles and titles

An example to avoid is that of Sir William Lucas in *Pride and Prejudice*, who, having merely received a knighthood for civic duties, counts himself an habitué of the Court of St James's, and an expert on the ways of the aristocracy.

It is, however, useful for all ladies and gentlemen to have a basic knowledge of the system of styles and titles – if only to avoid such social 'Blunders' as Anna Austen's belief that the courtesy title

'The Honourable' would be cited when introducing the younger son of a peer.

Anyone who wishes to find out details concerning the nobility should consult the authorities on the subject (the *Peerage* and the *Baronetage* published by Debrett), which contain biographical details of the British aristocracy and baronetage. The Authoress herself was able to answer her niece's question as to whether a fictional title used in her novel actually existed, by checking in these works. They are, of course, the favourite reading of the self-important Baronet Sir Walter Elliot, in *Persuasion*, who never tires of looking up his own family entry in 'the *Baronetage*'.

Rule 6. *Always show restraint on meeting and greeting*

The formalities to observe, on being introduced to a stranger, or greeting a friend, are simple and straightforward enough. Indeed, it

is a point of English decorum (let us not say reserve!) that they should be so: flamboyances and flourishes, such as kissing hands &c., are best left to other nationalities.

A lack of ostentation does NOT indicate any lack of feelings. The Authoress makes this clear. When describing the reunion of Mr Knightley and his brother, in *Emma*, she writes,

> 'How d'ye do, George?' and 'John, how are you?' succeeded in the true English style, burying under a calmness that seemed all but indifference, the real attachment which would have led either of them, if requisite, to do everything for the good of the other.

Between sisters, or ladies of equal age, or rank, within a family, a kiss on the cheek is acceptable; gentlemen and ladies on affectionate terms may exchange a cordial handshake (such as takes place between Emma and Mr Knightley, just before his brother's appearance). In almost every circumstance, a gentleman will make a slight bow, a lady, a restrained curtsey, on meeting. The depth and duration of these gestures should be in proportion to the honour they are intended to confer. A slight inclination of the head, a swift bob of the knees, will suffice between – say – the Miss Bingleys and the Miss Bennets, Mr Elton and Miss Smith, John Thorpe and Catherine Morland. A more exaggerated gesture – such as the 'twist of the head', which is the 'coxcomb' Robert Ferrars' favoured greeting to Elinor Dashwood – is a sign of foppery, rather than good manners; and the constant 'low bows' bestowed by Mr Collins, in fawning on his patrons, are as ill-judged, and obsequious, as those of his pretentious father-in-law Sir William Lucas, who longs to impress his acquaintances with his knowledge of breeding and the manners of the great.

Rule 7. *Take care in the correct use of names*

Outside the realm of titles, the use of names is by no means complicated – but is liable to admit of many 'Blunders'. The essential rules to bear in mind are these:

The eldest daughter in a family is simply 'Miss X', using her surname only. Any sisters are 'Miss (then the Christian name) X'. Thus, in *Pride and Prejudice*, the heroine's elder sister is

Miss Bennet, while she is Miss Elizabeth Bennet, and her sisters Miss Mary, Miss Kitty and Miss Lydia. It is, by this token, incorrect to speak of the Authoress as 'Miss Austen'; that title belongs to her sister Cassandra, the first-born. She is properly styled 'Miss Jane Austen', or to intimates, 'Miss Jane'.

In friendships among people of the same sex, certain intimacies will be permitted; men of equal rank (particularly those who have been schoolboys together) may refer to one another, familiarly, by surnames alone. For a female to do this – as Mrs Elton does, in *Emma* – demonstrates not merely 'Ease' of manners, but gross impertinence.

Even towards parents, the respectful terms 'Sir' and 'Ma'am' will regularly alternate with the more familiar 'Papa' and 'Mama'; and it is entirely usual, among all classes, for elder married couples to address one another by their titles: 'Lady Bertram', 'Mrs Bennet', &c. – though the younger husbands and wives (as the Authoress's novels demonstrate) are increasingly likely to use each other's Christian names. It is, of course, wholly improper for a lady and gentleman, until they are engaged, to use one another's Christian names, except within the family. Willoughby's presumption in addressing the younger Dashwood sister simply as 'Marianne' without being formally engaged to her, demonstrates his disturbing tendency to flout Society's Rules – in this, as in greater matters. Even young ladies should not be too prompt to call one another by their first names: and indeed, the heroine of *Northanger Abbey*'s elegant future sister-in-law remains 'Miss Tilney' to her, throughout much of the novel.

Only a woman of the presumption and low breeding of a Mrs Elton would take it upon herself to transgress this code – which, like all Society's rules of conduct, is intended to safeguard the dignity of others and ensure a mutual sense of respect.

Chapter the Third

CALLING AND CONVERSATION

The morning was chiefly spent in leaving
cards at the houses of Mrs Jennings' acquaintance, to inform them of her being in town.
Sense and Sensibility, Chapter 27

Mr Darcy, and Mr Darcy only, entered the
room . . . Said Charlotte, as soon as he was
gone, 'My dear Eliza, he must be in love with
you, or he would never have called on us in
this familiar way.'
Pride and Prejudice, Chapter 32

'I know gentlemen do not like morning visits',
says chatty Miss Bates in *Emma*: and it may be
with candour confessed that ladies do not

always enjoy them either. None the less, the business of paying, and receiving, social calls is one of the essential duties of day-to-day life, in both town and country; and the rules which govern 'calling' must be carefully observed, by both sexes.

Where calls are concerned, 'Morning' relates to the entire period between breakfast and dinner (which may be from, say, 10 a.m. to as early as 3.30 or 4 p.m. in rural or old-fashioned circles). During these hours, once housekeepers have been instructed, letters written and shopping done, it is customary to 'wait upon' friends, relations and acquaintances – to welcome a new neighbour, pay compliments to a bride, enquire after the afflicted, or discuss a recent ball; in short, to maintain, through the exchange of family news and general civilities, the fine network of contacts and obligations around which the 'Polite World' inevitably revolves.

While such visits are intended to give pleasure to all concerned, they are, of course, subject to a strict code of Manners (as the Authoress was obliged to remind her niece in 1814, when advising her on her attempts at writing a novel set in Society).

Calls must be paid and returned promptly. They must be neither too brief nor overly long. They should show a due attention to differences both of rank and of sex. With this last particularly in mind, they should, at all costs, do nothing to hazard the reputation of a lady. It may be recalled that the indiscreet visits paid by Lady Caroline Lamb (albeit in disguise) to the lodgings of Lord Byron, in 1812, did as much to confirm Society's talk of scandal and adultery as any other of her 'Horrible Blunders'.

Rule 1. *A lady may not call upon any gentleman*

This rule is demonstrated in the opening chapter of *Pride and Prejudice*. Mrs Bennet, mother of five marriageable daughters, has to cajole and coerce her reluctant husband into visiting their rich, new, bachelor neighbour, because, as a respectable lady, she may not call on him herself. As she insists,

My dear, you must indeed go and see Mr Bingley when he comes into the neighbourhood . . . for it will be impossible for us to visit him, if you do not.

Until this introductory visit is paid, no deeper connection between the families – from dinner invitations to marriage proposals – can result.

''Tis an etiquette I despise', Mr Bennet protests when Mr Bingley's return, later in the novel, causes the whole 'calling' procedure to commence again. None the less, it is an etiquette to which Good Manners – and Compliments – constrain him to conform.

Even the immoral but well-mannered Mary Crawford in *Mansfield Park* is obliged to abide by this rule. When longing to see the novel's hero, Edmund Bertram, she can only persuade him, through a mutual friend, to call on her. In his words,

He had seen Miss Crawford. He had been invited to see her. He had received a note from Lady Stornaway, to beg him to call.

The Authoress herself, when wishing to discuss professional matters with her publisher,

John Murray, had to request him to 'wait upon' her.

Rule 2. Be sure to leave cards

All ladies and gentlemen should carry 'Calling Cards' printed with their name and title, to which may be added, by hand, their current address, 'At Home' details &c.

(Decorative cases for these may be acquired from jewellers such as Gray's of Sackville Street, where Elinor Dashwood, in *Sense and Sensibility*, sees Robert Ferrars ordering an ornamental toothpick case.)

On arriving in Town, or a new neighbourhood, it is customary to leave cards on friends, relations and acquaintances, existing or hoped for, thus indicating that a call has been paid, and a return visit will be acceptable. Leaving one's card is a mark of courtesy; whether or not to return the compliment is for the person thus 'waited on' to decide.

Cards are placed on a salver in the entrance hall, to show the family (and the world) who has called. Regrettably, when wishing to avoid an encounter with Marianne Dashwood, while preserving 'the air of a cool common acquaintance', the deceitful Willoughby watches to ensure that she is not 'at home' before leaving his card – in what some might term a cruel 'charade'.

At Bath, new arrivals are listed in the famous visitors' 'Book', situated in the Pump Room for anyone to consult – as Catherine Morland does in *Northanger Abbey*, when seeking the Tilneys' address. This, of course, also enables vulgar persons to leave cards where they may not be welcomed. This is a 'Horrible Blunder'! As self-important Sir Walter Elliot complains, on removing to Bath in *Persuasion*:

> Everybody was wanting to visit them. They had drawn back from many introductions, and still were perpetually having cards left by people of whom they knew nothing.

Rule 3. Pay, and return, calls promptly

Never delay a visit when it is due. Any sense that an expected call is paid with reluctance will, naturally, cause offence.

Commenting on an early chapter of her niece's novel, in 1814, the Authoress warned

> Your G.M. (Grandmother) is more disturbed at Mrs F.'s not returning the Egertons' visit sooner than anything else. They ought to have called at the Parsonage before Sunday.

While staying in London, in *Pride and Prejudice*, Jane Bennet is troubled by Miss Bingley's slowness in returning her call. After four weeks 'she could no longer be blind to Miss Bingley's inattention'. Eventually she tells her sister, Elizabeth,

> When she did come, it was evident that she had no pleasure in it; she made a slight formal apology for not calling before, said not a word of wishing to see me again . . . When she went away, I was perfectly resolved to continue the acquaintance no longer.

By not repaying this call, Jane effectively ends the friendship. No further invitations will be extended between the parties; and if they meet in public they need not acknowledge one another.

Rule 4. Do not call too briefly

Any visit should last for at least fifteen minutes. When the heroine of *Emma* seeks to detach her protégée Harriet from her friendship with the worthy Martin family, she ensures that the girl's next visit, though unavoidable for the sake of Good Manners, shall show that 'it was to be only a formal acquaintance'. The upshot, under Emma's unfortunate influence, is that 'The style of the visit, and the shortness of it, were then felt to be decisive. Fourteen minutes . . . !'

Naturally, nothing will end an acquaintance more decisively than the pretence of being 'not at home' to visitors when 'waited on'. Young Catherine Morland, in *Northanger Abbey*, is most distressed when, having called to apologise to Miss Tilney for an imagined slight, she is turned away.

She gave her card. In a few minutes the servant returned, and with a look that did not quite confirm his words, said . . . that Miss Tilney had walked out.

When the lady is then seen 'issuing from the door', Catherine could 'almost be angry herself, at such angry incivility'.

Rule 5. Visits of 'duty' must never be neglected

'Everybody who comes to Southampton finds it either their duty or pleasure to call upon us', the Authoress recorded ironically in 1804. Calls which may be considered a duty rather than a pleasure are those 'visits in form' which must be paid to the newly-married; the bereaved; and those in straitened circumstances, who are all too liable to feel themselves neglected.

Not to wait upon a bride is very remiss . . . This is a matter of mere common politeness and good breeding.

frets old Mr Woodhouse in *Emma*. He is correct. But Emma, his daughter, reflects,

It was an awkward ceremony at any time to be receiving wedding-visits, and a man had need be all grace to acquit himself well through it. The woman was better off; she might have . . . the privilege of bashfulness.

Visits to the bereaved require more delicacy, naturally. After the funeral of a young friend in Bath, in 1801, the Authoress wrote that she

Called without expecting to be let in, to enquire after them all. On the servant's invitation however I sent in my name, & Jane & Christiana . . . came to me immediately, and I sat with them about ten minutes.

People in reduced circumstances may be especially sensitive to the observance of the Rules of calling. Impoverished old Mrs Bates and her garrulous spinster daughter in *Emma* 'loved to be called on'; but Emma, knowing herself to be 'rather negligent in that respect', finds visiting them 'very disagreeable – a waste of time – tiresome women'.

Here, paying 'compliments' – in the sense

of showing good manners – is revealed not merely as an aspect of politeness, but of true humanity. Emma's neglect – such as all should avoid – is shown up by Mr Weston's injunction to his son to visit Miss Bates's niece Jane.

> Go today! Do not defer it. What is right to be done cannot be done too soon . . . She is with a poor old grandmother, who has barely enough to live on. If you do not call early it will be a slight.

Rule 6. Visits of 'pleasure' should be carefully judged

Among the most agreeable visits are those paid on the morning after a ball, at which the young ladies – and any gentlemen present – may enter with relish into the details of the night's entertainment: who danced with whom, who wore what, which couples seemed particularly interested in one another, &c.

It is good manners for an unattached gentleman to call on his principal partner of the night before, to enquire after her health and continue

"An unreserved conversation"

the acquaintance. However, while often being a source of particular interest and pleasure to all concerned, such visits should be undertaken with care: an overly eager call by any gentleman upon a lady may lead to unwarranted speculation.

The haste with which Mr Darcy comes to call on Elizabeth Bennet, when he is staying with his aunt and she at the adjacent vicarage, is indicative of more than usual attentiveness. Elizabeth's hostess, the vicar's wife Charlotte Collins, exclaims knowingly,

I may thank you, Eliza, for this piece of civility. Mr Darcy would never have come so soon to wait on *me*.

When the Authoress called on the aunt of her youthful suitor Tom Lefroy, soon after a ball in 1796, she reported,

He is so excessively laughed at about me . . . [that] he ran away when we called on Mrs Lefroy a few days ago.

N.B.: This 'Blunder' was remedied soon after when Tom Lefroy and his cousin George ('he is really very well behaved now') very properly returned the Austen sisters' call.

Rule 7. *Make polite conversation*

Too much 'ease' of manners, such as Mrs Elton displays, is ill-bred; her fulsome chatter about the Woodhouses' 'charming place', and 'extensive grounds' on first visiting them in *Emma*, for example, is intrusive rather than graceful. However, over-much shyness during a social visit may be no less taxing to others' politeness.

After calling on a neighbour, Lady Fagg, and her five daughters ('I never saw so plain a family!') with her niece Fanny in 1813, the Authoress reported 'It was stupidish: Fanny did her part very well, but there was a lack of Talk altogether'.

Where subjects of genuine mutual interest are lacking, it is a vital point of good manners to maintain a steady flow of small-talk, based on obvious rules of politeness.

Calls must always commence with enquiries after the respective families' health. These should not be uncomfortably protracted: in *Pride and Prejudice*, for example, Mr Collins' 'formal civility' is shown in its true light when he detains Elizabeth Bennet in the cold, on her arrival at his vicarage, 'some minutes at the gate, to hear and satisfy his enquiries after all her family'.

Nevertheless, paying compliments must involve such enquiries, and to omit them is a decided 'Blunder'. When diffident Edward Ferrars calls 'at a very awkward moment' in *Sense and Sensibility*, Elinor Dashwood is 'obliged to volunteer all the information about her mother's health, their coming to town, &c, which Edward ought to have enquired about, but never did.' Edward does, however, obey the 'Rules' sufficiently to ask 'Do you like London?' – the next polite conversational step. Mr Darcy, in a similarly unexpected and uncomfortable situation early in *Pride and Prejudice*, asks Lizzy Bennet coldly, while picking up a newspaper, 'Are you pleased with Kent?'

"Mrs Armstrong sat darning a pair of stockings the whole of my visit"

The best combination of sense and elegance in small talk is displayed by Frank Churchill, during his first call on Emma Woodhouse:

> Their subjects in general were such as belong to an opening acquaintance. On his side were the enquiries 'Was she a horsewoman? – Pleasant rides? – Pleasant walks? – Had they a large neighbourhood? . . . Was it a musical society?'

Rule 8. Occupy yourself, and your guests

A call may involve more than mere chit-chat. It is perfectly correct to offer refreshments to guests – such as the 'beautiful pyramids' of fruit served by Miss Darcy during Elizabeth Bennet's visit to Pemberley. If there are children in the household, they may be brought in by their nurse, and introduced: as the Authoress has observed in *Sense and Sensibility*, a child should always be of the company, during a call, to provide a focus for conversation and enquiries – and begin to acquire his or her own social graces.

A gentleman is at liberty to pick up a newspaper during a call, and scan it; for ladies, there

is always the option of 'working' – meaning, of course, needle-work. Visitors may avail themselves of the communal work-basket containing items of linen, such as collars for the gentle-men of the family, or babyclothes, or garments for the poor, which require fine or fancy hemming, 'making up', or smocking.

Delicacy is essential where such activities are concerned: mending such coarse items as underlinen is wholly unacceptable. Visiting an acquaintance at Lyme, Miss Armstrong, whom she described as 'considerably genteeler than her parents', the Authoress noted with amuse-ment,

Mrs Armstrong sat darning a pair of stock-ings, the whole of my visit. But I do not mention this at home, lest a warning should act as an example.

Rule 9. *When in doubt, talk of the weather*

The Authoress would freely admit that discussing others' follies, foibles and even troubles may – however deplorable – be among life's pleasures. In 1801, for example, she wrote 'The Wylmots being robbed must be an amusing thing to their acquaintance'.

As caustic Mr Bennet observes, in *Pride and Prejudice*, 'For what do we live, but to make sport for our neighbours, and laugh at them in our turn?'

However, scandal and gossip should be omitted from polite conversation, in public. Other topics to avoid in company naturally include religion and the Slave Trade: when Fanny Price seeks to question her property-owning uncle about this burning issue on his return from the West Indies, she is greeted with 'dead silence'. Any references to pregnancy or childbirth are coarse, and should be carefully side-stepped by the truly well-bred, as should intrusive comments on love-affairs. When Mrs Jennings teases Elinor Dashwood about her supposed admirer, all present are grateful for Lady Middleton's insipid observation that 'It rained very hard'. On this she is joined by the ever-courteous Colonel Brandon, in another instance of his characteristic good manners, 'and much was said on the subject of rain by both of them'.

Chapter the Fourth

DANCING AND DINING

We had an exceeding good ball last night.

Jane Austen, *Letters*, 1799

Why did you dance four dances with so stupid
a Man?

Jane Austen, *Letters*, 1801

'Every savage can dance', declares Mr Darcy in
Pride and Prejudice, in one of his most cutting
set-downs. But even he would be obliged to admit,
if pressed, that dancing is also regarded by almost
every civilised young lady, and many gentlemen,
as one of life's most agreeable pastimes.

'It may be possible to do without dancing
entirely. Instances have been known', the

Authoress observes in *Emma*. Nevertheless, opportunities to enjoy 'a pleasant ball now and then', whether in a public assembly room or private household, are eagerly sought after, and can generally be contrived, in most circles. Unfortunately, however, it should be admitted that not all those present will acquit themselves with equal skill and grace, or be entirely familiar with the Manners and correct procedures required in a ballroom. For them, and the Authoress's readers in general, a number of Rules and guidelines may be of benefit.

N.B.: The term 'Ball' may be applied not only to a formal, public affair, such as those which are held weekly in the Upper and Lower Rooms at Bath, but also to a private, informal gathering of a few couples brought together by invitation, in a friend's house.

Rule 1. Learn to dance – and to dance well

Many people are taught in youth, by a proficient family member or friend, the steps and 'Figures' of the popular dances: Reels, Country Dances, Quadrilles, the Cotillion, the Boulangeries, the German Waltz, and so on. Others – especially those new to good society, such as the Coles in *Emma* – may choose to take lessons from a professional Dancing Master. (Advertisements for these instructors can be found in most newspapers: *The Times; The Bath Chronicle* &c.)

To dance badly is inexcusable, and may be classed as a 'Horrible Blunder'. Many readers will be familiar with the experience of Lizzy Bennet in *Pride and Prejudice*:

> Mr Collins, awkward and solemn, apologising instead of attending, and often moving wrong without being aware of it, gave her all the shame and misery which a disagreeable partner for a couple of dances can give.

The best pattern for all gentlemen to observe is Mr Knightley in *Emma*, with his 'firm, upright' stance, and 'natural grace'. As the heroine, Emma, notes with pleasure, 'His dancing proved to be just what she had believed it to be, extremely good.'

For ladies, Fanny Price's style in *Mansfield Park* is the ideal: her admirer Henry Crawford pictures her 'gliding about with quiet, light elegance, and in admirable time.'

"Not handsome enough to dance with!"

Rule 2. A gentleman may not ask a lady to dance with him without a formal introduction

'No one can ever be introduced in a ballroom', says Lizzy Bennet sarcastically. The opportunities for increasing one's circle of acquaintance through introductions to eligible new partners are, of course, among the principal pleasures of any ball, public or private.

The proper procedure for seeking an introduction is demonstrated by Mr Bingley in *Pride and Prejudice*, as Mrs Bennet reports:

> He seemed quite struck with Jane as she was going down the dance. So he enquired who she was, and got introduced, and asked her for the two next.

His friend Mr Darcy, by contrast, shows an offensive degree of pride, and lack of Manners, by declining Mr Bingley's offer of introducing him to Elizabeth Bennet, with the 'put-down', or rebuff, 'She is tolerable; but not handsome enough to tempt *me*.'

Rule 3. Having refused one gentleman, a lady may not accept another's invitation

Courtesy, and concern for others' feelings, will dictate that a lady may only decline a gentleman's polite invitation to dance on the grounds of fatigue, or some other reasonable excuse. It would be hurtful to his dignity, should she then 'stand up' with another partner – however preferable!

As a result, many a lady will find herself either obliged to dance with an unappealing partner, or, unless he finds another partner, sitting down for the next two.

This is Elizabeth Bennet's fate, when pestered by Mr Collins at the Netherfield Ball in *Pride and Prejudice*: 'Though he could not prevail with her to dance with him again, [he] put it out of her power to dance with others.'

The Authoress herself had a similarly frustrating experience at a local Assembly Room ball of 1801: in a letter to her sister, she confessed to

Sitting down two dances in preference to having Lord Bolton's eldest son for my partner, who danced too ill to be endured.

Rule 4. A lady may not invite a gentleman to dance

It is for the gentleman to choose his partner: if no invitation is forthcoming, the ladies present must sit – however disconsolately, or frustratingly – at the side of the room, with their chaperones, family and female friends. 'It went to my heart that the Miss Lances . . . should have partners only for two', the Authoress wrote after a local ball in 1808.

On informal occasions, if there is 'a scarcity of men', two ladies may choose to dance together. Should a child with good manners, and good connections, have been permitted to join the company, it is a charming act of courtesy for a lady to 'stand up with him', or her – as Emma Watson does, in the Authoress's unfinished novel, *The Watsons*, with the well-behaved, young Master Blake, who has been looking forward to the occasion and practising his steps, and comes properly equipped with white gloves.

Rule 5. Observe the rules of precedence, with tact

The highest-ranking lady present will stand at the head of the first set, and lead off the dancing, unless a ball is given in honour of another person – a young lady making her debut in society, for instance (such as Fanny Price in *Mansfield Park*, who is alarmed by the honour) or a new bride (such as Mrs Elton in *Emma*, who insists on it, to the annoyance of her social superior, Miss Woodhouse).

Rule 6. Make amusing conversation while dancing

'Do you talk by rule then, while you are dancing?' Mr Darcy asks Elizabeth Bennet. While she has intended to tease him out of his studied coolness by her playful questions, there is a point to them. Couples who 'stand up'

together in a ballroom are expected to make conversation; and may thereby strike up a warmer acquaintance – as Henry Tilney and Catherine Morland do in *Northanger Abbey*, waiting in line, facing one another, before the moment comes to dance up the 'set' and perform the required steps and movements of 'hands across', &c.

Rule 7. *Observe the rules of sitting down*

When the required two dances – or 'two next' – end, the gentleman should escort his partner back to her chaperones. It is for him to join her party and be introduced, not vice versa – as Emma Watson gently explains to her juvenile partner, who wishes to introduce her to his companions.

If supper is about to be served when a dance ends, the gentleman must remain with his current partner and escort her into the supper-room.

At no point (contrary to some ill-informed, modern dramatists' notions!) will any lady be left to wander a ballroom alone, or mingle freely in a crowd: she will at all times be under the care either of her partner or her chaperone.

Rule 8. Do not intrude upon the dancers in a ballroom

A point that all should note is that – even while waiting in line to move up the set – dancers are expected to pay attention to one another, not to those gentlemen who may choose to stand behind them and chat. After a ball in 1798, the Authoress reported that a friend named Mr Calland 'stood every now and then behind Catherine and me to be . . . abused for not dancing'.

Sir William Lucas takes it upon himself to converse with Elizabeth and Mr Darcy while they are dancing; and Henry Tilney, in *Northanger Abbey*, is downright annoyed with oafish John Thorpe when he commits the same ballroom 'Blunder'.

Rule 9. Make the effort to enjoy dinner parties

Dinner parties are not always a source of unmixed pleasure, either to host or guests. While young, unattached gentlemen and single ladies may welcome them as opportunities to dine well and make new acquaintance, more domesticated older gentlemen may share the amazement of Mr John Knightley, in *Emma*, that any man would choose 'the efforts of civility and the noise of numbers' over 'the tranquillity and independence of his own fireside'. The Authoress, writing from Bath in 1801, referred dispiritedly to 'Another stupid party last night'.

For some hosts, they appear scarcely more pleasurable. Lady Catherine de Bourgh's invitation to the Collins party indicates that 'She felt herself so dull as to make her very desirous of having them all to dine with her.'

This invitation may none the less be regarded as a compliment: it is quite usual to ask guests merely to arrive after dinner, to share in the tea or coffee which will then be served. There is usually some enjoyment to be had from the entertainment then offered: music, cards, some impromptu dancing &c.

Rule 10. *Attend to your neighbour's needs at table*

Ladies and gentlemen may go into dinner at a private house grouped as they wish; but once seated (with the most distinguished lady on the

The pleasures of cards

host's right, the superior gentleman, likewise, to the right of the hostess) the formalities of making polite conversation to one's neighbour, ensuring that ladies' plates and glasses are refilled, &c., must be attended to. It is *not* polite to talk behind one guest's back to another – as Mrs Jennings does in *Sense and Sensibility*, to tease Marianne about Willoughby; still less so to shout down the table, as Mrs Bennet does in *Pride and Prejudice*, to pass on news of the latest London fashions.

It is not proper to suggest that the ladies of the house have had any part in the cooking beyond instructing the housekeeper. This 'Blunder' on the part of Mr Collins is somewhat tartly answered by Mrs Bennet with 'her daughters had nothing to do in the kitchen.'

The head of the household, seated at the end of the table, will, however, carve for the company.

Rule 11. *After dinner the ladies must withdraw*

The ladies withdraw at the end of dinner, while the men remain at table, to enjoy port and, it is generally assumed, conversation on such topics as sport, politics and farming, as opposed to the predictable feminine subjects of children, dress and servants.

Any gentleman with a particular interest in one of the ladies is likely to hate 'sitting long', as does Frank Churchill – eager to rejoin Jane Fairfax in the drawing room, where the tea and coffee are being served. (As tea is so expensive, it will have been brought in in a locked 'caddy', and mixed by a trusted family member.) Those other guests who have been 'invited to tea' will arrive at this stage.

Rule 12. Assist in the after-dinner entertainment

'I hate tiny parties, they force one into constant exertion', the Authoress has candidly confessed. While it is possible to lose oneself in a throng, in a small group a good deal of conscious attention to others' needs must be paid, after dinner as well as during it, in the interest of good manners.

Cards are more than likely to form part of any evening's entertainment. It is thus proper

for all ladies and gentlemen to acquaint themselves with the different games, and be ready
to join in whichever the senior persons present
opt for – from the fashionable piquet, or loo, as
played by the Bingleys at Netherfield, to the
more staid and traditional whist, or 'pool of
quadrille' often favoured by older people. While
it is correct for a guest to decline if he or she
believes the others will be 'playing high' – for
stakes beyond his or her means – it is typically
uncivil of Marianne Dashwood to refuse to join
Lady Middleton's rubber of casino, saying
abruptly, 'You know I detest cards.'

Music will almost certainly be called for.
Any lady with a talent for the pianoforte, or
harp, should oblige the company, both by solo
performance and by accompanying others in
singing. Here, a balance must be struck; all
who wish to demonstrate their accomplish-
ment should be pressed to do so – but should
have the tact to limit their display. Anne Elliot,
in *Persuasion* – though the most talented
performer present – shows the ultimate good
manners by listening politely to others, and
when called upon herself, volunteering merely
to play country dances, so that the rest of the

company may enjoy that other most popular evening entertainment – 'an unpremeditated little ball'.

Rule 13. Return invitations promptly

Guests must ensure that they repay hospitality promptly: they will not be invited again until this has taken place.

Socially punctilious Lady Middleton, in *Sense and Sensibility*, asked by her jovial husband to include certain friends in a party, replies, 'It could not be done. They dined with us last.'

'You and I . . . should not stand upon such ceremony', her mother, jolly, vulgar Mrs Jennings, responds; to which her other son-in-law replies cuttingly, 'Then you would be very ill-bred.'

Which of those present here represents the best Manners, it may be left to the reader to decide.

Chapter the Fifth

DRESS AND TASTE

Mrs Powlett was at once expensively and nakedly dressed.

Jane Austen, Letters 1801

Elizabeth saw, with admiration of his taste, that it was neither gaudy nor uselessly fine.

Pride and Prejudice, Chapter 43

For young Fanny Price, contemplating her first ball in *Mansfield Park*, 'the "how she should be dressed" was a point of painful solicitude'; and so it is for many people, on many occasions. How to appear 'elegant' without seeming too fine; how far to follow friends' advice, or the latest ideas in the fashion magazines; which colours, fabrics, trimmings and accessories to choose, to follow the mode without overstepping the bounds of suitability and propriety, are all questions to be carefully considered.

The admirable Mr Brummell – lately Captain Brummell of the 10th Light Dragoons – has clearly established the connection between dress and manners. Elegance of appearance – as he has so notably shown – should reflect elegance of mind. Contrary to what some ill-informed or ignorant critics have suggested, the Authoress's novels contain almost no detailed references to clothing – bonnets, ballgowns, or otherwise, or even clear descriptions of her characters' features and looks. None the less her readers should be in no doubt as to the 'elegance', or lack of it, displayed by each person portrayed. To those familiar with the fashions of the day, the merest hints – Fanny Price's simple white gown and amber cross, Mrs Elton's 'purple and gold ridicule'*, Isabella Thorpe's 'coquelicot ribbons', &c. – should convey all that is necessary.

---

* Ridicule: A reticule, or bag.

As with every other aspect of Manners, and good breeding, in matters of dress restraint is all: and with this in mind, the following basic rules regarding dress and taste may be of some assistance to readers.

Rule 1. *Appear unconcerned as to dress*

Dress is at all times a frivolous distinction, and excessive solicitude about it often destroys its own aim.

The Authoress's oft-quoted comment in *Northanger Abbey* is only half-ironic. It is proper for a gentlewoman to take a close interest in fashion: to wish to appear 'elegant', and to express both her personality and her taste in her mode of dressing. Even modest Fanny Price, in *Mansfield Park*, is happy to find herself 'deep in the interesting subject' with her undeniably 'elegant' rival in love, Miss Crawford; and the Authoress, in her private letters, reveals considerable 'solicitude' about fashion, writing frequently of changes in head-dresses, sleeve-lengths, corsetry &c., the choice of new gowns*, and her own opinions on others' attire. Nevertheless, her fictional characters would seem to support Mr Brummell's famous dictum: that the truly elegant (gentlemen especially), having dressed with care, should then seem oblivious to their own appearance.

Rule 2. *Avoid finery and show*

In all the Authoress's novels, too much attention to fashion or finery is invariably a hallmark of the ill-bred or bad-mannered. The 'foolish coxcomb' Robert Ferrars in *Sense and Sensibility*, for example, is 'adorned in the first style of fashion'; and the exemplar of under-bred affectation, pretentious Mrs Elton in *Emma* ('Insufferable Woman!'), is notable for the 'studied elegance of her dress'.

In her love of 'lace and pearls' Mrs Elton is at odds with impeccably-mannered Fanny Price, in *Mansfield Park*, who prefers 'a plain gold chain,

---

* A 'gown' may refer to a dress-length of material, and not a made-up garment.

perfectly simple and neat' over a more ornate 'necklace of gold, prettily worked', to wear with her brother's cherished gift of an amber cross, at her first ball. Here, Miss Price directly reflects the Authoress's own taste. She and her sister were given similar crosses, in topaz, by a beloved sailor brother in 1801. Some years later, the Authoress reported to Cassandra from London, 'I have bought your Locket . . . it is neat & plain, set in gold'.

Keeping up with fashion's changes should never outweigh personal judgement – whatever ladies' style magazines, such as *La Belle Assemblée*, *Ackermann's Repository*, &c., may dictate. When brilliant colours are in vogue, they should be adopted with discretion: seeing friends in new mantles (or outergarments) in 1809, the Authoress told her sister 'You will value . . . the modest propriety of Miss W's taste, hers being purple, and Miss Grace's scarlet'.

Rule 3. *When in doubt wear a white gown*

'A woman can never be too fine while she is all in white', pronounces Edmund Bertram in *Mansfield Park*, to reassure Fanny Price that she is not overdressed for her first dinner-party. His judgement is correct. A simple white dress in, say, a light muslin or fine silk, will always appear both fashionable and suitable; and any truly elegant female should own 'a large stock of white gowns' – as does the Authoress's sister, Cassandra. In a letter of 1801, the Authoress joked to her, 'I begin with the hope . . . that you often wore a white gown.'

'Put on a white gown. Miss Tilney always wears white' is a rare, and useful, piece of advice given to young Catherine Morland in *Northanger Abbey*.

Having chosen such a gown, avoid any temptation to over-adorn it. In the interest of fashion the fabric may be subtly detailed: Fanny Price's, for example, is woven with 'glossy spots' – but Mrs Elton's notion of 'putting such a trimming as this to my white and silver poplin' shows that she has entirely misunderstood the principle of taste on which this fashion is based.

Rule 4. *Use cosmetics with restraint*

A fair, unblemished complexion may be in vogue; but in pursuit of this, the use of cosmetics is generally not recommended. The heavy skin-whitening pastes of former times, involving ingredients such as white lead and mercury, are now mercifully discredited; and even for those who, like Mrs Clay in *Persuasion*, are afflicted with freckles or other disfigurements, nothing stronger than Gowland's Lotion (advertised in the *Bath Chronicle*, and elsewhere) should be hazarded – and then applied sparingly.

A light use of rouge is permissible, particularly in the 'first circles': Sir Walter Elliot in *Persuasion* suggests this for a once-attractive but ageing family friend, Lady Russell: 'If she would only wear rouge, she would not be afraid of being seen!'

On observing a well-known society 'adulteress' in Bath, the Authoress reported, 'She was highly rouged, & looked rather quietly & contentedly silly, than anything else.'

"A woman can never be too fine while she is all in white"

The young, and the naturally elegant, would be well advised to follow the heroine Anne Elliot's example, and use 'nothing at all' by way of cosmetics.

Astute readers of the Authoress's works will note that a lightly tanned complexion may even be attractive. Of one of her most beautiful characters, Marianne Dashwood, she states, 'Her skin was very brown'; and when Miss Bingley in *Pride and Prejudice* censures Elizabeth Bennet for seeming 'so brown and coarse', Mr Darcy coolly replies that she is 'rather tanned' as a result of 'travelling in the summer', which, to his elegant eye, is evidently more a recommendation than not.

Rule 5. Style your hair with care

Every gentlewoman should be able to style and dress her own hair, in the absence of a lady's maid or professional hairdresser. The services of the latter may indeed be a mixed blessing: from London, in 1813, the Authoress wrote,

[Mr Hall] curled me out at a great rate. I thought it looked hideous, and longed for a

snug cap instead, but my companions silenced
me by their admiration.

Wearing 'a snug cap', in light muslin, is always
a safe solution to unruly hair – though the fash-
ion-conscious young (including the Authoress's
own nieces and nephews) generally consider this
ageing, if not a downright fashion 'Blunder'.

Outlandish hairstyles, though distressingly
prevalent, will inevitably arouse comment, and
are sad 'Blunders'. The mode for gentlemen
(having abandoned wigs) to wear their own
hair, unpowdered, natural and short – often
brushed forward in a quiff – is now too general
to be remarked on, even by the conservative.
Ladies, however, should not adopt this fashion.
The Authoress was disconcerted by her daring
niece Anna's 'sad cropt head', noting that 'the
cutting off her hair is very much regretted'.

Too much attention to one's hair, as to all
aspects of dress, is, of course, not compatible
with proper dignity. Thus, when Frank
Churchill in *Emma* conceals his true errand in
London under the excuse of going to get his
hair cut, he is called 'a coxcomb' and laughed
at for 'foppery and nonsense'.

Rule 6. *Do not dress immodestly*

Although the 'present fashions' are so evidently influenced by classical statuary – flowing Grecian lines, high waists, bare arms, flat-heeled footwear, &c. – these echoes of antiquity should not outweigh discretion. True 'elegance' is not achieved through transparent fabrics or naked limbs and bosoms, as the Authoress has frequently (and not always charitably) pointed out. A Miss Langley was described by her in 1801 as 'Like any other short girl with a . . . fashionable dress & exposed bosom.'

On another occasion she wished her sister 'A pleasant party tomorrow, and not more than you like of Miss Hatton's neck'.

And once she wrote of seeing at a ball 'So many dozen young Women standing by without partners, & each of them with two ugly naked shoulders!'

Of course the décolletage will always go up and down, as the mode dictates: in 1814 the Authoress herself 'lowered the bosom' of an evening gown, and further emphasised the bust with plaited ribbon; but she welcomed the

"A very elegant young woman"

change in corsetry of 1813, which meant, she wrote,

> That the stays now are not made to force the bosom up at all; *that* was a very unbecoming, unnatural fashion. I was really glad to hear that they are not to be so much off the shoulders as they were.

It was an unfortunate coincidence that the Austens' acquaintance Mrs Powlett who had appeared at a party 'both expensively and nakedly dressed' should have a kinswoman who subsequently faced further exposure, in the Press, as an Adulteress.

Rule 7. *Dress should always be suitable – and practical*

What is fitting for Town wear may not be correct for the Country, in terms of dress. Ill-mannered Miss Steele, in *Sense and Sensibility*, displays her ignorance of London ways and good manners when, on meeting Elinor Dashwood in Kensington Gardens, she ends their conversation with

La! If you have not got your spotted muslin on. I wonder you was not afraid of its getting torn.

For a morning walk in this Royal Park, where the *'ton'* (or elegant) would promenade and meet, Elinor has, with characteristic good taste, opted to wear a light, fine and fashionable dress. Out for a morning walk in the country, she would naturally choose a gown of sturdier stuff, in which, if need be, she could climb stiles and jump puddles (as Lizzy Bennet does, unconcerned for appearances, in *Pride and Prejudice*).

For all the undoubted impact of sporting clothes on men's formal attire, it would be wholly incorrect for Mr Willoughby to wear his shooting jacket (however 'becoming') in Town, or Mr Knightley his stout leather gaiters, or Emma Woodhouse the galoshed 'half-boots' in which she takes her strolls down country lanes.

N.B.: Even in the realms of fashion, sense should prevail over sensibility.

Rule 8. *Be cautious with comments on others'* *dress – compliments included*

It is only natural for ladies to take an interest in others' attire. The Authoress herself has, in private, frequently praised or criticised other females' fashion sense – as when, for example, she wrote of a Miss Seymour, at Bath,

> Neither her dress nor air have anything of the Dash or Stilishness which the Browns talked of . . . indeed, her dress is not even smart.

However, whether charitable or otherwise, such comments should be exchanged only with close family and intimate friends. To question – or even compliment – anyone else, in person, on the details of dress may be regarded as impertinent.

Miss Steele's scrutinies of Marianne Dashwood's toilette are the height of bad manners, ranging from 'the price of every part' of her dress to 'the number of her gowns', and concluding with an examination into the value and make of her gown, the colour of her shoes, and the arrangement of her hair.

Miss Bates, in *Emma*, by contrast, shows the correct form when — while clearly admiring Emma's looks at a ball — she says 'Must not compliment, I know . . . that would be rude'.

Chapter the Sixth

THE SUBJECT OF MATRIMONY

Oh Lizzy! Do anything rather than marry without affection.

Pride and Prejudice, Chapter 59

Do not be in a hurry: depend upon it, the right Man will come at last.

Jane Austen, *Letters*, 1817

Where matters of love and marriage are concerned, a strict adherence to the formal codes of good manners is a matter of the highest importance. Any form of 'leading on' a potential admirer; trifling with another person's affections; imprudent freedom with a member of the opposite sex; or calculated encouragement of attentions without affection for the pleasure of a conquest or the hope of an advantageous marriage, must be deplored, and will have no place in the life of a rational, right-thinking man or woman.

'She goes on now as young ladies of seventeen ought to do, admired and admiring' the Authoress once wrote of an attractive young acquaintance; and certainly it is quite natural for ladies of all ages to seek to make themselves agreeable to eligible gentlemen, and enjoy their attentions. But modesty, and a proper regard for the sensitivities of others, should combine to direct any lady, or gentleman, of character and principle in their dealings with each other. Society's Rules on such points are designed not to hinder, but to protect; and those who flout them – as do hotheaded Marianne Dashwood in *Sense and Sensibility* and (to an incomparably worse degree) Lydia Bennet in *Pride and Prejudice* – are hazarding their entire future happiness, along with their reputations.

Rule 1. Never be indecorous, or indiscreet

Any kind of impropriety, in the form of over-familiarity, overt flirting, or other behaviour which may arouse comment, should be scrupulously avoided. A woman's reputation for virtue is one of her most precious possessions: as Mary Bennet (albeit sententiously) observes in *Pride and Prejudice*, 'Loss of virtue in a female is irretrievable . . . one false step involves her in endless ruin.'

Worldly, cynical Mary Crawford's comment in *Mansfield Park* – 'There is undoubtedly more liberality and candour on those points than formerly' – may be true of the tainted world of London society, which is her own moral *milieu*, with all its false values; but every honourable person in both the Authoress's life and her novels rejects any such notion. Only sad and silly women (ignorant Isabella Thorpe, in *Northanger Abbey*; coarse Mrs Clay in *Persuasion*; &c.) would be so foolish, and misguided, as to risk all for what they might regard as love – or worldly advantage. When would-be social rebel Marianne Dashwood learns of her admirer Willoughby's heartless

seduction of Colonel Brandon's niece, and
realises what her own fate might have been, she
can only reflect, with compassionate tears, on
'the wretched and hopeless situation of this
poor girl'. Virtuous Fanny Price, in *Mansfield
Park*, responds predictably with 'modest
loathings' and sleepless nights to the revela-
tion of her cousin Maria's adultery with Mr
Crawford. But even merry, free-thinking
Elizabeth Bennet is deeply affected by the
thought of her sister Lydia's conduct in living
with Mr Wickham outside marriage:

> 'It is most shocking indeed', replied Elizabeth
> with tears in her eyes, 'that a sister's sense of
> decency and virtue in such a point should
> admit of doubt.'

Rule 2. Avoid open shows of affection

The Authoress herself, while deploring overt
flirtation, was happy to make teasing references to it – as when she reported to her high-
minded sister after a ball in 1796, at which she
had danced several times with her admirer, Tom
Lefroy,

"Admired and admiring"

I am almost afraid to tell you how my Irish friend and I behaved. Imagine to yourself everything most profligate and shocking in the way of dancing and sitting down together.

With the risks of more serious gossip in mind, Elinor Dashwood feels obliged to warn her own sister that her imprudently romantic behaviour with Willoughby, such as driving off in his open curricle alone with him, allowing him to use her Christian name, &c., 'has already exposed you to some very impertinent remarks'.

Rule 3. Maintain your dignity

Even within the family circle, ladies should behave with decorum. Maria Bertram in *Mansfield Park* is most unwise to engage in amateur theatricals: as an engaged woman, she should not be seen uttering love speeches to, let alone embracing, a gentleman other than her intended husband.

All forms of touching a member of the opposite sex should be kept to a minimum. Putting a lady's shawl about her shoulders, or assisting her to mount a horse, enter a carriage &c.,

is of course entirely acceptable; and it is indeed absolutely correct for a gentleman to take a lady's arm through his, to support her while out walking. (Kissing – even for an engaged couple – is, of course, out of the question.)

The relaxed, playful manners of Elizabeth Bennet – however charming – occasionally cause her to be accused of 'impertinence'; and only her innate judgement saves her from indulging in flirtation with Mr Wickham. 'Without supposing them . . . very seriously in love', her 'elegant, intelligent' aunt, Mrs Gardiner, notes, nevertheless, that 'their preference of each other was plain enough to make her a little uneasy'.

To be seen running after officers, like the younger Bennet girls, is a great 'Blunder'; although it may be admitted that the sight of a gentleman in uniform – such as Mr Wickham's scarlet 'Regimentals' – is enough to turn many a lady's head. 'There is no resisting a Cockade, my dear', admits a character in one of the Authoress's early works, *The Watsons*; while Mrs Bennet, in *Pride and Prejudice*, sighs tenderly, 'I remember the time when I liked a red coat myself, very well.'

"There is nothing like your officers for
captivating the Ladies"

Rule 4. Do not indulge in matchmaking

It is natural to wish to see friends happily married; and even, on occasion, to seek to bring two eligible people together. This should, however, only be undertaken with great care (as the meddlesome heroine of *Emma* comes to realise).

The Authoress herself has been the subject of such well-meant interference: on moving to Chawton, where the curate was then a single man, she wrote, with amusement, 'Depend upon it . . . I *will* marry Mr Papillon, whatever may be his reluctance, or my own.'

And indeed, she permitted herself, on several occasions, to speculate about possible marriages for friends and relations. When her close friend Miss Sharpe, former governess at Godmersham, became governess to the children of a widower, Sir William Pilkington, she could not resist confiding, in a letter to her sister,

> I do so want him to marry her . . . Oh Sir Wm! Sir Wm! how I will love you, if you will love Miss Sharpe.

The desire to see her beloved niece Fanny, who consulted her at length on her tangled love affairs, happily married, led to such comments (in private to Cassandra) as 'He is such a nice, gentlemanlike, unaffected sort of young man . . . I think he may do for Fanny'.

Rule 5. Do not be 'bent on marriage'

'You know, we must marry. I could do very well single for my own part', admits a character in *The Watsons*; another, in the same novel, observes 'To be so bent on Marriage, to pursue a Man merely for the sake of situation – is a sort of thing that shocks me; I cannot understand it'.

To wish to marry, and enjoy the sweets of a happy, companionate union, and the blessing of children, is natural, and even laudable: indeed the Authoress wrote to Fanny in 1817, 'I do wish you to marry very much, because I know you will never be happy till you are'.

However, it is regrettable that women so often have been brought up to the 'trade' of 'coming out' in Society, with no other purpose in view but an eligible marriage. This is, in the main, because, for those with no independent fortune, there are so few other prospects for them in life, other than becoming a governess, or, as a character in *The Watsons* sighs, a 'Teacher at a school; and I can think of nothing worse'.

None the less, the pursuit of marriage for its own sake, however understandable, is to be deplored. The Authoress has stressed on more than one occasion, 'Anything is to be preferred or endured, rather than marrying without Affection.'

Women who can think, or talk, of little else but 'setting one's cap at a man', 'making a conquest', or 'catching a beau' are displaying, not merely bad manners, but a lack of moral judgement.

Rule. 6 *Do not encourage unjustifiable expectations*

Every gentleman – and lady too – should pay close attention to the dangers of showing over-much interest in a member of the opposite sex. As the heroine of *Mansfield Park* states with unusual vehemence, 'I cannot think well of a man who sports with any woman's feelings'.

The Authoress, counselling her niece, Fanny Knight, felt obliged to warn, regarding one admirer, 'You certainly *have* encouraged him to such a point as to make him feel almost secure of you'.

It is wholly 'ungentlemanlike' of Frank Churchill to conceal his secret engagement to another lady by showing 'persevering attention' to Emma Woodhouse. The perfect conduct of Mr Knightley, in all his dealings, shines the brighter by contrast: in Emma's sober words,

> Mr Knightley is the last man in the world who would intentionally give any woman the idea of his feeling more for her than he really does.

Rule 7. Pay heed to the rules of engagement

Outside the family, a lady and gentleman may not correspond with one another, unless they are engaged. The fact that Marianne Dashwood writes to Willoughby is taken by her mother and sister to be positive proof that he has proposed honourable marriage to her. It is only by going in person to the local Post Office to collect her letters that Jane Fairfax in *Emma* is able to conceal her secret engagement with Frank Churchill: he could not be writing to her under any other circumstances.

An engagement to be married is solemn and binding. Should the gentleman have a change of heart, it is wholly unacceptable for him to break his word, and withdraw the offer of marriage: this would be to the lady's discredit, as well as disappointment.

Edward Ferrars obeys this Rule to the letter by standing by his (much regretted) engagement to the grasping and unworthy Lucy Steele: she, in contrast, demonstrates a shocking lack of propriety by holding him to it. The heroine, Elinor, reflects,

Self-interest alone could induce a woman to keep a man to an engagement, of which she seemed so thoroughly aware that he was weary.

Rule 8. Marry only for the right reasons

'To marry for money, I think the wickedest thing in existence', announces young Catherine Morland in *Northanger Abbey*; and, while not necessarily endorsing that statement to the full, the Authoress assumes her readers will agree with the sentiment. No 'gentlemanlike', honourable man, or lady possessing elegance and delicacy, would allow themselves to be influenced by considerations of wealth or rank when choosing a partner in matrimony.

(The Authoress was, of course, not intending to be taken seriously when – weighing up the merits of her niece Fanny's rival suitors – she admitted, 'I like Chilham Castle for you', in reference to young Mr Wildman's family seat.)

It is, however, only fair to acknowledge that all right-thinking people would wish to marry suitably.

Rule 9. Refuse a marriage proposal with dignity

There can be very few ladies who are not gratified to find themselves the object of a gentleman's regard. To be so singled out will add greatly to any woman's 'consequence' among her friends. It is, however, most improper, and indelicate, to encourage hopes of matrimony which will not be fulfilled.

Should matters proceed to an unwanted proposal, this must be refused with the greatest delicacy, and attention to the gentleman's feelings.

To maintain the dignity of both parties, the lady must (whatever her private sentiments) refer first to her consciousness of the honour bestowed on her. Elizabeth Bennet's refusal of Mr Collins in *Pride and Prejudice* follows the correct pattern:

> Accept my thanks for the compliment you are paying me. I am very sensible of the honour of your proposals, but it is impossible for me to do otherwise than decline them.

Should the gentleman not have the taste and delicacy to desist at this point, more emphasis may be brought to bear: faced with Mr Elton's unwanted, importunate offer of marriage, the heroine of *Emma* resorts to stating icily, 'I have no thoughts of matrimony at present.'

While self-effacing Fanny Price – shocked at Henry Crawford's proposal in *Mansfield Park* – tries to stop him with 'This is a sort of talking which is very unpleasant to me.'

Should a gentleman be obtuse or importunate enough to continue to press his suit, a lady may be justified in using stronger words.

'My feelings in every respect forbid it. Can I speak plainer?' Elizabeth Bennet finally exclaims to Mr Collins. And faced with Mr Darcy's first, 'ungentlemanlike' proposal, she feels justified in ending her rejection by calling him, 'The last man in the world whom I could ever be prevailed on to marry'.

She will, of course, come to regret this lapse in good manners.

Rule 10. *Accept a marriage proposal with grace*

To accept a gentleman's formal addresses will require even more composure, and sense of propriety. The ideal exchange in this most delicate of situations is surely that of Mr Knightley and his intended bride Emma: in the Authoress's discreet account, his proposals are made in

'Plain, unaffected, gentlemanlike English, such as Mr Knightley used even to the woman he was in love with'. He tells her, 'If I loved you less, I might be able to talk about it more.'

And in response: 'What did she say? Just what she ought, of course. A lady always does.'

There could be no better distillation of the combined rules of Good Manners.

Chapter the Seventh

THE FAMILY CIRCLE

The repose of his own family circle is all he wants.

Mansfield Park, Chapter 21

Though the Children are sometimes very noisy . . . I cannot help liking them.

Jane Austen, *Letters*, 1817

Whatever the circumstances in which she has been brought up, any woman is likely to dream of acquiring an 'establishment' of her own. Some, in pursuit of this, will even settle for a less-than-happy marriage – so that, by substituting a husband's authority for that of her parents, she may enjoy 'the sweets of house-keeping', with charge over almost every aspect of her own, and her family's, daily life, from the choice of servants, and the upbringing of children, to the supervision of her kitchen and garden, and the provision of hospitality to guests. Even Charlotte Lucas, having married the tedious Mr Collins in *Pride and Prejudice*, for the 'pure and disinterested desire of an establishment', is acknowledged by the very differently-minded Elizabeth Bennet to have found a measure of happiness in 'her home and her housekeeping, her parish and her poultry'.

Rule 1. Know who has charge

In the interest of a smooth-running household, it is of the first importance to consult the tastes and wishes of the Master of the house. Only a female of the unusual notions of a Mrs Godwin (known to many as Mary Wollstonecraft), who appears, with her radical persuasions, to flout every convention of normal womanly virtue, would question this state of affairs – but she is fortunate in having a husband as 'raffish' as herself.

Naturally, while all right-thinking persons will recoil at Mrs Elton's coy usage, in *Emma*, of the phrase 'My lord and master' for her husband, any woman of sense will acknowledge that a little artfulness is useful in ensuring that a husband's happiness coincides with her own in domestic arrangements – Charlotte, for example, encourages Mr Collins to stay outside working in the garden as late and as long as he pleases.

Rule 2. Create an atmosphere of order and harmony within the home

'To sit in idleness over a good fire in a well proportioned room is a luxurious sensation', the Authoress wrote on one occasion after dining at a friend's grand house. To enjoy what she has termed 'the Elegance & Ease & Luxury' of life in a great country mansion – from the real-life Godmersham to Mr Darcy's fictional Pemberley – is a taste natural to most people. None the less, in any well-run household however small (such as the Austens' own rented cottage, Chawton, or the seaside lodging inhabited by the gallant Captain Harville in *Persuasion*) a due attention to orderlness, tidiness and propriety will create an agreeable atmosphere, and give a pleasurable impression to guests.

It is not the cramped size of her parents' house at Portsmouth which distresses Fanny Price, and makes her homesick for well-regulated Mansfield Park, but the disorder and disregard for others' needs which she finds there. Banging doors, rampaging children and insolent servants all contribute to the 'Horrible Blunder' which is bad housekeeping.

Rule 3. Never be put off from showing hospitality by limited accommodation

'Pray, where did the boys sleep?' the Authoress enquired with interest, after hearing of a visit from her nephews to crowded Chawton during her absence. Any difficulties posed by lack of rooms, space or even beds should never be permitted to interfere with the demands of hospitality to family or friends. Something can always be contrived.

At both Steventon Rectory and Chawton cottage the Authoress and her sister always shared a bedchamber; and when necessary, like most of their contemporaries, they have been happy to share a bed. This is always a good solution to shortages of accommodation, for persons

"Delightful Sport—!"

of the same sex: it may even be an agreeable opportunity for friendly conversation.

In *Persuasion*, the Harvilles display good manners of the most admirable kind when, following Louisa Musgrove's accident on the Cobb at Lyme, they put her up in their own small home, making light of the inconvenience thus:

> Putting the children away in the maid's room, or swinging a cot somewhere', they could hardly bear to think of not finding room for two or three besides.

Rule 4. Provide occupations and pastimes for guests (and family)

It is generally taken for granted that all gentlemen enjoy country sports – shooting in particular – while ladies (who do not take part in these manly activities) are assumed to find agreeable occupation in caring for their children, walking, riding, practising the pianoforte or harp, drawing, needlework, and, of course, reading. A selection of these resources and pastimes should be on hand at all times for the entertainment of both family members and friends.

A well-stocked library is seen by many as essential in any home. (The Authoress's father, in his relatively modest vicarage at Steventon, owned some 500 volumes.) For some gentlemen, a billiard room may seem even more desirable. Of these rival domestic pleasures, the Authoress wrote from Godmersham in 1813,

> The Comfort of the Billiard Table here is very great. It draws all the Gentlemen to it whenever they are within . . . so that my Brother, Fanny & I have the Library to ourselves in delightful quiet.

Tom Bertram, in *Mansfield Park*, is most uncivil in his remarks as to his father's deficiencies as a parent and host in possessing a 'horribly vile' billiard table.

It is important to keep children happily occupied. Pet animals, such as a parrot, a cat, or a dog such as Lady Bertram's pampered pug, are always of use, to be played with, or 'teased'. Making paper ships and bombarding them with horse-chestnuts; learning to 'knot' rabbit-nets; playing at shuttlecock and battledore, or practising the art of 'cup and ball' are among the

Authoress's other recommendations, tried and tested on her own beloved nephews.

N.B.: When other ideas fail, children may often be left to create their own amusements. Catherine Morland, for example, in *Northanger Abbey*, not only enjoys 'cricket, baseball . . . and running about the country' with her siblings, but also, simply, 'rolling down the green slope at the back of the house'.

Rule 5. *Attend to dietary needs – and even food fads*

To have charge of the household is to assume responsibility for the diet, and culinary require-ments, of all its occupants and guests. These must be observed with consideration in the interests of both health and Good Manners.

Simple, nourishing, home-grown food is at all times recommended; but modern 'fads' and personal preferences should be attended to.

The question of dietary difficulties arises notably in *Emma*; old Mr Woodhouse, persuaded (with the help of physicians) that many basic foodstuffs, from pork loin to baked apples, may represent health hazards, insists on denying his guests many simple culinary pleasures: watering their wine; refusing them delicacies such as sweetbreads; permitting only small portions &c. Only through his daughter's good offices in replenishing plates and glasses, and seeing to their real needs, are visitors allowed to enjoy his well-meant hospitality to the full. 'I hope I am not often deficient in what is due to guests', is Emma's gentle, and justified, summing-up.

Pretentious Mrs Elton, in the same novel, may claim credit for being shut up, for half an hour with her housekeeper, arranging menus; but Emma sets the proper example of Good Manners, and hospitality, from the liberality of her entertainment at home, to the courtesy with which she shares her family bounty with those less fortunate. Her neighbourly generosity in sending the best cuts of a newly-killed pig to the impoverished Bates family is mirrored by Mr Knightley's determination to send them a plentiful supply of apples. Such attention to others' needs is, of course, a major proof of 'delicacy', and innate Good Manners.

Rule 6. *Bring children up responsibly*

Where a happy domestic life is concerned, almost nothing is of greater importance than the application of proper 'Method' in bringing up children.

Jane Bennet in *Pride and Prejudice*, when left in temporary charge of her young cousins, the Gardiners' children, sets the right example, by simply 'teaching them, playing with them, and loving them'. This is similar to the 'Method' adopted by the Authoress in caring for her nephews, the elder Knight boys, after their mother's death in 1808; when, having encouraged them to shed tears freely if they wished, and ushered them to church, she cheered them up with all manner of distractions and treats. Entertaining a friend's daughter, Catherine Foote, in 1807, she reflected with amusement, 'What is become of all the Shyness in the World?' – having been a shy child herself. However, the modern young (as she was pleased to observe) possess a 'ready civility', which, in the interest of Good Manners, is surely preferable. The Authoress took particular pleasure in showing this 'little visitor' the 'Treasures of my Writing desk' as she stood 'talking away at my side'.

Rule 7. Do not over-indulge children

While harshness should have no place in bringing up children, over-indulgence is equally to be avoided. By placing their children's wishes over their guests' comfort, families such as the Dashwoods and Middletons, in *Sense and Sensibility*, demonstrate bad manners, and lack of proper concern for others.

John Dashwood pleads his son's wish to see the wild animals at the Exeter Exchange as an excuse for not calling – as he should have done – on his half-sisters, on their arrival in town; Lady Middleton, in the same novel, allows her infants to run riot – plaguing guests and bullying one another – to the point where even mild-mannered Elinor Dashwood is driven to exclaim,

"While I am at Barton Park, I never think of tame and quiet children with any abhorrence"

I confess . . . while I am at Barton Park, I never think of tame and quiet children with any abhorrence.

Rule 8. *Do not dwell upon matters of maternity and childbirth*

Where the delicate matters of Motherhood and 'lying-in' are concerned, the Authoress has made her opinions clear: they should be mentioned with restraint.

To be in a certain 'Condition' will be the inevitable lot of many women, and is, of course, no easy situation: on learning of her would-be novelist niece Anna's latest pregnancy, in 1817, the Authoress wrote 'Poor Animal; she will be worn out before she is thirty', and of her sister-in-law Fanny, wife of Charles Austen, she wrote with sympathy, before one confinement, 'Little Embryo is troublesome, I suppose'.

She would also remark of this much-loved sister-in-law, and her childbearing: 'From that quarter, I suppose is to be the alloy of her happiness'.

However, the birth of a child must always be treated as a matter of joy. In polite circles, it is correct to announce these events in the Newspapers: thus, in *Sense and Sensibility*, the birth of Mrs Jennings' first grandchild is, via the press,

announced to the world . . . a very interesting and satisfactory paragraph, at least to all those intimate connections who knew it before.

Rule 9. Retain a sense of 'elegance' as far as possible, when lying-in

Children are, as the Christian Marriage Service proclaims, central to the fulfilment of human relationships, and creation of a happy family and home life. None the less, it is incumbent upon every woman to undertake the arduous burden of procreation with as much attention to Good Manners, and 'elegance', as possible –

to encroach as little as she can, in other words, upon the goodwill and tolerance of her friends and relations.

All ladies, and gentlemen too, will feel for any woman facing the ordeal of childbirth. In 1798, after recording that two acquaintances had died in the process, the Authoress added, referring to a sister-in-law who was about to be confined, 'We have not regaled Mary with this news.'

She was, however, not above making unkind comparisons in her friends' and relations' manners of managing the experience. Mary Austen seemed distracted and untidy, with threadbare curtains, while Elizabeth Knight – surrounded, admittedly, by all the comforts of 'East Kent wealth at Godmersham – was able to appear a vision of contented and elegant maternity.

There is every reason for a woman to manage all aspects of childbirth and motherhood with regard to the demands of good manners and the welfare of others, as well as herself. After visiting family friends, the Rev. Henry Dyson and his wife, in 1801, the Authoress wrote fastidiously, 'The house seemed to have all the comforts of little Children, dirt & litter. Mr

Dyson looked wild, & Mrs Dyson as usual looked big.'

Such a household is scarcely conducive to harmony or propriety. All ladies would do well to remember that 'where a home is a scene of contentment', gentlemen are more likely to acquire 'the strong domestic habits' of uxorious Mr John Knightley, in *Emma*.

Chapter the Eighth

THE ASSISTANCE OF SERVANTS

Mary's promised maid has jilted her and hired herself elsewhere.

> Jane Austen, *Letters*, 1800

You should always remember the coachman and horses.

> *Mansfield Park*, Chapter 25

In no sphere of daily life is there a greater need for strict attention to the demands of 'Politeness and Propriety' than in the treatment of servants.

Virtually everyone in possession of an income of £100 a year or more employs servants, lives surrounded by them and is, in some degree, dependent on them. Without servants to cook, clean, wait at table, wash clothes, drive carriages, tend gardens and answer doors, society could scarcely function effectively. As the Authoress's novels continually – if discreetly – demonstrate, these beings are a constant presence in every aspect of existence; and it is incumbent upon both their employers and themselves to pay the utmost attention to the Rules of conduct which govern their respective situations and duties.

The following general Principles may offer some useful guidance: –

Rule 1. The number of servants kept must be in proportion to the master or mistress's income, not aspirations

It is possible, but highly unusual, to manage without so much as a kitchen-maid. The Authoress exclaimed in a letter of 1796 over a young couple of her acquaintance who were living at Portsmouth:

in the most private manner imaginable . . .
without keeping a servant of any kind. What
a prodigious innate love of virtue she must
have, to marry under such circumstances!

On their own modest income of £500 per
annum, the Authoress, her widowed mother and
unmarried sister were able to employ, at
Chawton, the 'two maids and a man' who also
make up the frugal, but genteel, household of
Mrs Dashwood and her daughters in *Sense and
Sensibility*. By contrast, on learning in the same
novel that her cousin Lucy is to marry on a
mere £100 a year, practical Mrs Jennings calcu-
lates

Two men and two maids indeed! – as I talked
of t'other day: No, no, they must get a stout
girl-of-all-works.

For people of fortune, such as Mr Darcy in
Pride and Prejudice, with his £10,000 a year,
and General Tilney in *Northanger Abbey*, an
appropriate household may be assumed to
include a steward, a butler, a housekeeper, liver-
ied footmen, chambermaids, housemaids,

kitchenmaids and their underlings (washer-women, bootboys, &c.). Out-of-doors, below the bailiff, there would be gamekeepers, the team of coachmen, grooms and stableboys, gardeners, estate workers, &c.

On seeing round the 'domestic offices', or kitchen regions, at Northanger, unworldly vicar's daughter Catherine Morland is positively awed by

The number of servants continually appearing . . . Wherever they went, some pattened* girl stopped to curtsey, or some footman in dishabille** sneaked off.

---

* Pattens: Stout, iron-based clogs.
** Dishabille: With livery unbuttoned – improperly dressed.

"A trollopy-looking maidservant"

Rule 2. Servants must be properly trained and supervised

The behaviour and working standards of servants will reflect – for good or ill – on their employers. When the door of the Prices' house at Portsmouth is opened by 'a trollopy-looking maidservant', it is clear what poor housekeeping lies within, due to the mistress's laxity:

> The tea board never thoroughly cleaned, the cups and saucers wiped in streaks, the milk a mixture of motes floating in thin blue, and the bread and butter growing every minute more greasy even than Rebecca's hands had first produced it.

It is vastly to Mr Darcy's credit, and raises him in Elizabeth Bennet's esteem, that his great estate at Pemberley is a model of efficient management, and his devoted house-keeper proves to be 'a respectable-looking, elderly woman, much less fine, and more civil, than [Elizabeth] had any notion of finding her'.

Rule 3. Servants should know their place, and keep to it

While taking a proper pride in themselves and their work, servants should not seek to appear above their station. The hauteur displayed towards Elizabeth by 'the two elegant ladies' who are the Bingley sisters' personal maids reflects their mistresses' pretensions and manners. Even off duty, servants should not attempt to ape their betters, in either dress or demeanour. A housekeeper in *Mansfield Park* has 'turned away two housemaids for wearing white gowns'; and even the lax Mrs Price is discomposed if she should see Rebecca pass by with a flower in her hat. Mrs Musgrove, in *Persuasion*, expresses the problem when she complains of her daughter-in-law's nursemaid, Jemima.

> She is always upon the gad . . . and she is such a fine-dressing lady that she is enough to ruin any servants she comes near.

Rule 4. Show respect towards servants

Differences of rank are almost as keenly felt among servants as they are by their employers, in their own circles, and should be as carefully upheld – not least through the forms of address.

While a mere maid, such as the Prices' Rebecca, or the Bates's Patty in *Emma*, will be known by her Christian name alone, those with authority within the household may expect the dignity of a surname. Thus Lady Bertram's personal lady's maid in *Mansfield Park* is 'Chapman', or 'Mrs Chapman'. Most importantly, a housekeeper must always be addressed as 'Mrs', according her the status of a married woman, even if she is single.

Manservants, likewise, are 'James', 'Thomas', &c.; but the butler at the Authoress's brother's estate, Godmersham, is 'Johncock', or even 'Mr Johncock' – as in one of her letters: 'I did not mean to eat, but Mr Johncock has brought in the Tray, so I must.'

To mock, mimic or otherwise belittle servants or their families, as does Mrs Norris in *Mansfield Park*, is unworthy and undignified – and a sign of bad manners, not superior gentility.

That said, it is only to be expected that employers will from time to time permit themselves a little gentle humour in private on the topic of servants' well-known  ways and foibles. The Authoress herself – as an astute observer of human follies in general – joked to her sister, before removing to Bath in 1801,

We plan having a steady Cook, & a young giddy Housemaid, with a sedate, middle-aged Man, who is to undertake the double office of Husband to the former & sweetheart to the latter. No Children of course to be allowed on either side.

Rule 5. *Establish a bond of mutual regard*

With servants who are loyal, trustworthy and hard-working, the ideal relationship is one of mutual esteem, as well as respect – which may lead to many years of faithful service. Endeavour to earn their good opinion: as Elizabeth Bennet justly remarks after meeting Mr Darcy's housekeeper, 'What praise is more valuable than the praise of an intelligent servant?'

Mr Knightley's cordial, man-to-man treatment of his bailiff in *Emma* may cause Emma herself to refer, with a hint of pique, to 'his dear William Larkins', but it shows the master/servant relationship at its best; and it is underscored by the declaration of their well-bred neighbour Miss Bates, 'William Larkins is such an old acquaintance! I am always glad to see him.'

A similar instance, of a somewhat different nature, is given by the Authoress herself, referring to a manservant in a letter of 1804:

James is the delight of our lives . . . My mother's shoes were never so well blacked before, & our plate never looked so clean. He waits extremely well, is attentive, handy, quick and quiet . . . He can read, & I must get him some books.

Likewise, one of James's successors is mentioned as 'my own dear Thomas'; and another, William, is described as 'a good-look-ing Lad, civil & quiet'.

N.B.: A point of the utmost delicacy may perhaps be touched on here. There can be no grosser impropriety, or greater transgression of every rule of morality, let alone Manners, than any form of guilty connexion between master (or worse, mistress) and servant. Such matters do occur, both in life and literature, and indeed feature prominently in the works of two of the Authoress's own favourite novel-ists, Fielding and Richardson; but – it need scarcely be stated – they have no place in her own. As she notes at the conclusion of *Mansfield Park*, 'Let other pens dwell on guilt and misery'.

Rule 6. Never be over-familiar with servants

Because they perform so many intimate tasks, from preparing food and nursing children to brushing hair, assisting with dressing &c., it is easy for the unwary, or underbred, master or mistress to make a confidante, or even an ally, of a favoured servant. This should be avoided at all costs. It will lead to a diminution of the employer's authority – and will encourage the servant to assume a privileged interest in matters which are none of his or her concern. (Instances of this have regrettably been known even in royal circles, both past and present, throughout the centuries.)

In *Sense and Sensibility*, inquisitive tradesman's widow Mrs Jennings encourages her maid to discover from rakish Willoughby's groom where he and Marianne Dashwood went in his curricle, and then supposes by implication all that took place between them. And in *Pride and Prejudice*, when Mr Bingley returns to the neighbourhood, undignified Mrs Bennet, as indiscreet with inferiors as with her equals, 'through the assistance of servants contrived to have the earliest tidings of it'.

In a household where prying eyes and gossiping tongues are encouraged, no employer's secret can ever be safe. Thus, when Mrs Bennet's youngest daughter Lydia brings shame on the Bennet household by eloping, her discreet and elegant sister Elizabeth reflects sadly,

Was there a servant belonging to it who did not know the whole story before the end of the day?

"I dare say he often hears worse things said"

Rule 7. Be guarded: servants have ears

Because the servants in any well-ordered establishment, public or private, are trained to be as
quiet and unobtrusive as possible, it is easy at
times to overlook their presence. When Fanny
Price and her brother are reunited at Mansfield
Park, for example, their meeting has 'No
witnesses, unless the servants chiefly intent upon
opening the proper doors could be called such'.

It is important, however, to be mindful on all
occasions that even the most loyal – or appar-
ently disinterested – may pass on what they see
or hear, for their own pleasure or even profit.

When Lydia Bennet announces, over lunch-
eon at an inn, that she has 'capital news' to
reveal 'about a certain person', her wiser sisters
hasten to dismiss the waiter – to which the
noisy Lydia imprudently responds,

> That is just like your formality and discretion
> . . . I dare say he often hears worse things
> said than I am going to say.

While gossip about the Bennet family will
be of interest only in their own neighbourhood,

for those in more elevated circles, information from servants may lead to revelations in the newspapers, which are, regrettably, only too ready to pay for salacious items about the aristocracy, and other celebrated persons.

In *Mansfield Park*, adulterous Maria Rushworth puts herself 'in the power of a servant', in this case a lady's maid, and in consequence is exposed when a newspaper announces,

> A matrimonial *fracas* in the family of Mr. R. of Wimpole Street; the beautiful Mrs. R. . . . having quitted her husband's roof in company with the well known and captivating Mr. C.

Disgraceful as such revelations may be, however, the Authoress herself has been known to read them. In 1808 she wrote of a dashing acquaintance's elopement,

> This is a sad story about Mrs Powlett. I should not have suspected her of such a thing . . . A hint of it, with initials, was in yesterday's *Courier*.

Rule 8. Consider the coachman

A gentleman's carriage and horses are among his most valuable possessions: they, and his family, will be entrusted only to a coachman of impeccable steadiness, skill and sobriety. The coachman's opinions as to the state of the roads, the welfare of the horses, &c., should be respected, and his comfort considered, as the Authoress's novels have frequently shown.

It is bad manners to keep him waiting; likewise, at the end of an evening engagement, during which he will have seen the horses properly stabled, watered, &c., he must have them back in harness and the carriage punctually at the door, at the time stipulated. (Formal invitations may include, the phrase 'Carriages at . . .')

Even Mrs Norris in *Mansfield Park*, given to chivying and patronising servants, affects to show concern for the family coachman. To the more worthy, however, such courtesy should come naturally – as an aspect of a good heart, and good principles, as well as Good Manners.

IN CONCLUSION

'I dearly love a laugh', declares Elizabeth Bennet, at the outset of *Pride and Prejudice*; and many readers will surely endorse her light-hearted approach to life. Yet when – later in the novel – doubtful of Mr Darcy's love, and any hope of a happy outcome, she reflects 'It was necessary to laugh when she would rather have cried', her feelings may strike a still deeper chord. There can scarcely be a greater test of inner strength, and outward politeness, than the need to preserve the appearance of good humour in adversity; and it is proof of Elizabeth's innate worth that she is able to 'make her feelings appear what they were not', in such a situation.

Maintaining appearances is an essential aspect of Good Manners; but this is not to suggest that superficial graces, or false values, are in any way admirable. Mary Crawford's blithe comment, in *Mansfield Park*, 'Varnish and gilding hide many stains', reveals her for what she is: a heartless and cynical adventuress, corrupted by London society. The 'honest simplicity' of an artless Catherine Morland, or even Harriet Smith, is 'infinitely to be preferred'. Concealment and disguise of private emotions are often integral to polite conduct – but only when accompanied by 'active principle', 'rational judgement', and a good heart. Unbridled emotions, as displayed by romantically-minded Marianne Dashwood, may all too easily lead to incivility, and indiscretion: a far better example is set by Elinor Dashwood, of whom the Authoress states sympathetically, 'Her feelings were strong, but she knew how to govern them'.

Throughout the Authoress's works, the subject of Manners, whether good or bad, is a constant underlying theme. Compliments are paid;

charades revealed; horrible blunders perpetrated. Whatever changes the passing years bring, it is to be hoped that the role of Manners as an integral component of both life and literature will never cease to be of interest to the world at large.

A Note on the Author

Josephine Ross has written a number of books including, most recently, *Jane Austen: A Companion* published by Jane Austen's original publisher John Murray.

A Note on the Illustrator

Henrietta Webb is the co-creator of *Bad Hair* (published by Bloomsbury).